How To Manage Money

Understand Your Teen Better And The Definitive Handbook For Young Adults And Their Parents

(A Comprehensive Manual On The Art Of Financial Management)

Winston Cardinal

TABLE OF CONTENT

Introduction 1

What is the Significance of Budgeting? 45

Essential Measures for Attaining Financial Autonomy 66

Effective Strategies to Optimize Your Budget's Functionality 87

Selecting Your Vehicle for Passive Income Generation 102

The Importance of Exercising Prudence When Engaging in Online Passive Income Generation ... 113

Introduction

Throughout the years, I have had the privilege of establishing connections with tremendously accomplished individuals in the fields of finance and business. Thanks to the invaluable guidance of these individuals, my personal growth and acquisition of knowledge in these areas have enabled me to achieve remarkable success. I had the opportunity to observe, comprehend, and witness firsthand, as well as actively engage in the experience, learn from my own errors, and develop as a consequence. With that being stated, this guide aims to provide you with a systematic approach to attaining financial control and securing success in managing your finances.

Regarding the acquisition and execution of knowledge, I appreciate approaches that are minimalist, streamlined, and comprehensible as opposed to convoluted, perplexing, and captivating. Therefore, if you have a preference for intricate matters, this guide may not be suitable for your needs. This compilation of information aims to provide individuals with a streamlined, hassle-free, and effective approach to money management. Furthermore, one aspect that I truly appreciate about it is that it provides a means through which significant savings can be achieved while fulfilling both essential and desired obligations.

Numerous individuals would argue that the most effective approach to managing your finances is to diligently adhere to a budget. However, I would like to propose an alternative viewpoint. Budgeting bears resemblance to dietary restrictions: initially, one reduces consumption with the expectation of attaining a more desirable outcome. Nevertheless, over time, individuals may become aware of the extensive deprivation they subject themselves to, resulting in mounting frustration. The newly proposed strategy lacks enjoyment and adaptability. Though some positive outcomes may be observed, one may question its overall value. Subsequently, you reach a point of exasperation and dispose of all of it. The most valuable guidance is to cease the practice of budgeting your finances and instead commence managing them effectively. Precisely the procedure I will elucidate for you.

The most advantageous aspect of financial management

The primary advantage of effectively managing finances in my perspective is the attainment of personal liberty. Now one may perceive that the act of effectively overseeing one's finances could potentially impede personal autonomy, when in reality, it actively enhances it. Given that I am no longer subservient to my finances, but rather the one exerting control over them, I am experiencing a heightened sense of liberation. In all honesty, I am currently in a financial position where I am able to afford all my expenses without any difficulty. As a result, I am able to indulge in occasional short trips, invest in businesses I find appealing, contribute to charitable causes, further my education, and luxuriously shop for high-quality items. Additionally, it is worth emphasizing that my bills are consistently and punctually settled without fail. Yes, I am endowed with the freedom to exercise my financial resources to exert control over every aspect of my life, along with the aid of a robust infrastructure to facilitate my endeavors. Even more promising information pertains to the fact that if I am capable of achieving it, you have the capacity to accomplish the same objective, if not exceed it.

Spend your Money Wisely!

The financial challenges experienced by certain individuals arise from a lack of adequate income. However, a significant number of individuals encounter this challenge as a result of their inability to effectively manage their finances or due to a tendency to exceed their income. Nearly 73% of the American population deceases with outstanding financial liabilities.

1. Monitor Your Budget

In order to initiate the acquisition of prudent spending habits, it is imperative to attain a comprehensive understanding of the allocation of your financial resources. Establish a financial plan and meticulously monitor your income and expenditures. Once you have gained consciousness regarding the destination of your funds, you can commence exploring opportunities to allocate them more prudently.

2. Take into account the potential long-term benefits and drawbacks of purchases.

Frequent instances of impulsive buying are observed too often. While this may be deemed acceptable when procuring a one-dollar chocolate bar from the local supermarket, it poses a considerable issue when engaging in more substantial transactions. Prior to making a purchase, it is imperative to contemplate the long-term consequences it may have on your personal circumstances.

What is the remaining duration of its existence? Shall it lead to an augmentation of your debt? Does the benefit you will attain from it over its lifespan justify the expense?

These inquiries can be utilized to ascertain the true value of a potential purchase.

3. Exercise caution in utilizing your credit card solely for transactions within your financial means on a monthly basis.

Using credit cards does not necessarily result in financial loss. In light of these considerations, it is evident that they possess a considerable level of practicality, as numerous cards offer the added benefit of cash rebates for purchases.

Nevertheless, it is essential to utilize your credit card solely for transactions that can be settled in full by the end of each billing cycle.

If you settle your credit card debt in its entirety every month, you will not be subject to any interest charges, rendering it virtually indistinguishable from making purchases with cash.

Nevertheless, should you fail to settle your balance on a monthly basis, the accumulated interest could readily spiral out of control.

4. Cease your endeavors to make a favorable impression on others.

The average person often expends excessive amounts of financial resources in an attempt to uphold their outward image. A significant portion of our purchases, ranging from high-end automobiles to luxury fashion items, is motivated by the desire to impress others rather than being driven by our true personal preferences and affections.

But trying to "Keep Up With the Joneses" is expensive and pointless. Do not yield to the notion that it is necessary to expend funds in order to make an impression on others; instead, procure the possessions that bring you personal satisfaction.

5. Identify the Behaviors That Deplete Your Financial Resources

Once you commence the practice of meticulously tracking your expenses, it would be prudent to initiate an examination of any habitual tendencies that could potentially be adversely affecting your budget. These behaviors may encompass extravagant leisure activities, frequent dining at restaurants, excessive expenditure on clothing, or various other factors that deplete one's financial resources.

Once you have identified the habits that are significantly impacting your revenue, you can determine if they are truly essential.

6. Establish a Consensus on the Importance of Saving versus Making Purchases

Certain individuals possess an innate aptitude for diligently accumulating wealth and deriving satisfaction from the augmentation of their overall financial value. Additional individuals perceive money as an entity that necessitates immediate expenditure upon acquisition, wherein any alternative course of action instills a sense of opportunity lost.

If you happen to fall into the latter category, endeavor to cultivate a mindset that places emphasis on savings rather than expenditures. Ultimately, allocating financial resources towards items that are prone to rapid deterioration or diminishing appeal will invariably have a more adverse impact on your overall well-being than prioritizing investments or savings.

7. Commence your investments at an early stage.

Exercising judicious financial decision-making extends beyond simply abstaining from unnecessary purchases; it necessitates leveraging the accumulated savings to procure resources that contribute to the realization of one's monetary goals. Given this situation, the notion of initiating or concluding an investment portfolio at an early or limited stage holds no validity.

Allocating your funds towards trustworthy enterprises that demonstrate a potential for appreciation in the long run is invariably a wise utilization of your financial resources, irrespective of your age, limited investment capital, or ample financial standing.

CHAPTER TWO

HINDRANCES TO GROWTH

There exist impediments to progress, and one can surmount them solely by making the choice to venture beyond the confines of their comfort zone. Venturing beyond one's comfort zone entails assuming risks, which ranks among the key principles that shape the mindset of successful millionaires. Hence, the following are among the most significant impediments to growth:

Fear

Fear is occasionally valued and serves as a means of ensuring safety during necessary circumstances, yet it can also inhibit one's ability to take action when required. If you encountered a predicament requiring you to assume a risk and make a consequential decision, what were your emotional implications and how did you proceed? If the outcome was favorable and circumstances eventually resolved in a positive manner, I am confident that you experienced a sense of gratification. As individuals of the human species, it is acceptable to experience apprehension and prioritize personal safety. Nevertheless, opting to evade risk and adopt a cautious approach may not always yield advantageous outcomes.

Confront and surmount fear;

Regardless of your location, view fear as an emotion that consistently emerges to motivate personal growth. When venturing beyond your realm of familiarity, confront fear with courage by embracing it. Venturing beyond your comfort zone does not necessitate precipitous and audacious choices; rather, it entails fostering an open-mindedness towards embracing novel endeavors while refraining from letting fear compromise one's faculty of rationality. On occasion, one may accomplish a remarkable feat when faced with stress-induced circumstances and challenging problems. The purpose of such encounters lies in the potential for personal development that arises while overcoming these obstacles. Living beyond the boundaries of one's comfort zone inherently entails discomfort. You might experience a sense of discontentment with your current circumstances or feel dissatisfied with a current interpersonal relationship, among other possibilities. All of these uncertainties can be attributed to inquiries such as.... what do you want? May I inquire as to what it is you are seeking?

Lack of discipline

In the absence of careful planning, adherence to discipline, and a lack of commitment, the probability of losing one's financial resources increases significantly, indicative of imprudent handling. Adhere to a predetermined budget and maintain transparency in adhering to its confines, particularly if your intention is to preserve and augment your financial resources over an extended period. When embodying a sense of discipline, one is enabled to gradually achieve success and approach matters with due seriousness, thus avoiding the inadvertent neglect of crucial details. To clarify, in order to prevent these unfavorable circumstances, it is imperative that one generates and adheres to a meticulously designed budget. By doing so, one can effectively prevent excessive expenditures and establish financial discipline. Failure to engage in this practice will inevitably hinder the accumulation of wealth and result in an enduring cycle of living beyond means.

Adhering to a carefully planned budget and faithfully adhering to it, is the most effective approach towards achieving financial prosperity, albeit with the recognition that it may require a considerable investment of time. The primary objective is to effectively reduce expenses in order to allocate the resulting funds towards the accumulation of wealth.

Engaging in a counterfeit and consumerist lifestyle

When considering your aspirations and ambitions, it is essential to grasp the distinction between necessity and indulgence. Until you have attained your objective or come close to attaining it, it is imprudent to indulge in extravagance or embrace a materialistic lifestyle, such as desiring to follow the latest fashion trends or acquiring the newest gadgets, for instance. An extensive array of examples can be provided. Incorporating a lifestyle of simplicity ought to be integral to one's being; endeavors to refrain from excessive expenditure despite an increase in earnings should be paramount, with primary emphasis directed toward augmenting one's investments.

Debt

Undoubtedly, indebtedness can impede progress, albeit not universally. It is crucial to be aware that debt can quickly impede your progress towards financial objectives and accomplishments. Certain loans may be acceptable to pursue, such as those pertaining to running a small business or obtaining an education, among others. Please note that personal loans carry the highest interest rates among all types of loans. Therefore, it is advisable to avoid acquiring one if possible. Furthermore, it is highly advisable to minimize the usage of credit cards, as their repercussions can significantly deplete one's energy levels.

Inflation

This formidable adversary possesses the capability to eliminate all of your returns entirely, remaining concealed in the process, and it typically occurs on an annual basis. It is imperative to consistently ascertain that your investments possess the capability to yield returns that surpass the current inflation rate.

Errors related to Investments

Improperly organizing investment portfolios can hinder one's financial growth, posing as a formidable adversary. Ensuring the appropriate distribution of assets and conforming to investment instruments that align with your risk tolerance and investment time horizon should always be prioritized. Acquiring the appropriate expertise and equilibrium is a challenging and time-consuming endeavor, though exercising patience is crucial. When contemplating the future financial successes that lie ahead, endeavor to broaden your investment portfolio through comprehensive understanding.

Emergency

Unforeseen circumstances arise as emergencies, consequently, these situations can significantly influence your financial prosperity and development, encompassing instances such as abrupt job loss, illnesses, fatalities, accidents, and the like. Should an unforeseen event arise without the presence of an allocated emergency fund, you will undoubtedly encounter difficulties. When composing or designing your budget, it is important to allocate a portion for an emergency fund, as unforeseen circumstances may arise without warning. Insurance coverage is highly advantageous, and it is essential to seek the guidance of a proficient professional in order to ascertain the appropriate insurance policy that suits your needs while discarding those that are unsuitable. We kindly request that you make arrangements for the allocation of contingency funds.

Chapter 1 Start

It would be a deceitful assertion to state that money does not exert significant influence in our lives. By means of monetary resources, we are able to cover the cost of housing, settle our financial obligations, and even indulge in occasional vacations and luxuries that contribute to enhancing our overall standard of living.

Money management continues to be a persistent challenge, as numerous individuals experience a sense of being overwhelmed by the ongoing inability to maintain control over their financial circumstances.

Within the pages of this new publication, we will endeavor to explore strategies that can significantly enhance one's financial management skills through the adoption of straightforward yet effective methodologies.

Principles of fiscal management: essential convictions to relinquish

One prevalent error in the realm of inadequate financial management is the failure to attribute the appropriate significance to each individual expenditure.

Expenditure is not contingent upon our emotional well-being; therefore, engaging in spending does not necessarily result in feelings of happiness.

Upon careful consideration, it becomes evident that the purchase entails a restricted degree of emotional satisfaction that is fleeting in nature. In a similar vein, refraining from expenditures could potentially evoke a feeling of vexation in the event that our monetary means are inadequate to fulfill our expenditure requirements.

According to Megan Walls, the coach affiliated with the American organization Conscious Connection, the act of spending money has the potential to elicit a positive emotional response for individuals, which is subjective in nature. Emotions influence our perception of financial choices, evoking feelings of pleasure or dissatisfaction. When individuals engage in shopping to satisfy immediate desires or to alleviate emotional distress, they are often attempting to address a sense of emptiness stemming from loneliness or seek personal significance. "

In addition to this, it should be noted that engaging in excessive and compulsive spending, as well as excessively saving or refraining from spending altogether, are both incorrect and detrimental patterns of behavior. Hence, it is imperative that the handling of your finances be executed with precision and meticulous planning. Employing a well-defined strategy will enable you to ascertain the appropriate amount and timing of expenditures, thus promoting your financial tranquility.

Practical Strategies for Effective Financial Management: 7 Key Recommendations

1. Gather a comprehensive understanding of your financial condition.

One does not fully grasp the impact of one's financial decisions until one diligently documents all daily activities, including expenses, by sitting down at a desk or sofa.

So, all that is required is a small allocation of your time, the use of writing utensils or digital tools if you prefer, and your commitment to meticulously record all monthly income and expenses. To facilitate your assistance, it would be advisable for you to retain invoices pertaining to the most significant expenditures.

This will enable you to consistently maintain all the transactions in your portfolio readily accessible and prevent any unforeseen occurrence of the nature such as: "where has all the money I earned gone?" ".

2. Set SMART financial goals

After delineating your desired allocation of funds, it becomes imperative to establish financial objectives that embody the SMART criteria: specific, measurable, attainable, relevant, and time-bound.

I would like to present a demonstration of a SMART goal: It is imperative for me to fully repay a debt amounting to 5,000 by the conclusion of December 2022. As evident at first glance, this approach is inherently destined for success as it equips you with all the essential components to purposefully navigate towards a particular objective.

3. Establish your budget using the 50/30/20 guideline.

The 50-30-20 principle offers a convenient and efficient approach to financial management. In practical terms, the figures denote the proportions by which to distribute your funds and assign them to various objectives. The initial step you must take is to grasp the precise percentage into which your expenses categorize.

"In summary, the 50-30-20 rule can be succinctly expressed as:

- It is imperative that you allocate 50% of your salary for essential and obligatory expenditures at all times. As an illustration, the expense associated with renting unquestionably falls within a range of 50%.

- It is recommended that 30% of your salary be allocated for personal indulgences. More precisely, we are discussing pastimes and diverse areas of interest.

- A portion equal to 20% of the funds received should be allocated towards achieving various savings objectives.

4. Create an emergency fund

The prospect of the future invokes apprehension in individuals, particularly in light of the pandemic's stark reminder of the unforeseeable nature of events and the importance of vigilant preparedness. An essential resource that undoubtedly contributes to our sense of security is the presence of a contingency fund.

In the first instance, it is imperative to establish a well-defined notion of the precise amount of funds you intend to allocate to the aforementioned investment. With regards to this matter, it is crucial that the funds allocated are sufficient to meet the primary expenses you incur on a daily basis, such as rent and bills, for a maximum duration of 6 months.

In order to minimize expenditure and adhere to sound financial planning, it is essential to pinpoint and subsequently eradicate any superfluous expenditures.

One final but crucial measure to consider is refraining from yielding to the allure of easily getting entangled. Instead, it is highly advisable to allocate said funds into an emergency reserve that is designated solely for this intention. Indeed, should one choose to amalgamate funds designated for diverse objectives such as vacations, nuptials, and the like, it is possible to inadvertently access those funds without discrimination, thereby undermining all prior endeavors.

5. Enhance your income portfolio by establishing supplementary sources of revenue.

An effective strategy for enhancing your financial management skills is to adopt the practice of diversifying your sources of income. What are the reasons for you to engage in this action? By and large, one mustn't solely depend on their full-time income, particularly during periods of unpredictability.

The ability to rely on supplementary earnings will assist in overcoming forthcoming uncertainties.

6. Develop a proficient plan for repaying debts.

The debt? Undoubtedly, this obstacle poses a significant challenge to realizing your financial objectives and implementing efficient money management techniques. Consequently, it would be prudent for you to develop a strategic plan that can effectively evade commission expenses that may exacerbate your debt situation, and promptly settle them.

An effective recommendation that can greatly assist in meeting your obligations punctually is to establish automated payment methods.

Furthermore, it is important to determine an effective strategy for the proper management of debt repayment. Will you opt to prioritize the settlement of larger debts before addressing those of smaller amounts, or would you prefer to adopt the reverse order? When calculating the monthly payment, it is important to take into account that settling your debt earlier will result in reduced interest payments.

7. Mere willingness isn't sufficient for effectively managing your finances.

We collectively aspire to economize. The volition and drive play a crucial role in the attainment of any objective, yet regrettably they alone fall short. Frequently, it is a common occurrence that following the payment of rent, bills, and groceries, there remains no surplus to save.

This is precisely one of the rationales behind the necessity of setting aside your savings prior to incurring any personal expenses. How? It is advisable to implement the automation of allocating 20% of your salary towards diverse savings objectives.

In addition, you need not be concerned about the precise allocation of exactly 20% of your salary, as the percentage serves as a guideline, and the important aspect is fostering a consistent habit of saving.

Effective financial management: Investing can yield positive outcomes when executed with expertise.

If one desires to enhance their financial consciousness, contemplation of investing becomes inevitable.

Indeed, it is imperative that you acquaint yourself expeditiously with the practices of investment and savings. In addition, should you decide to engage in more frequent investment activities, you will have the opportunity to capitalize on additional earnings, which will exclusively enhance the performance of your portfolio.

There exist a plethora of investment instruments that enable the augmentation of one's returns. One may choose to place dependence upon conventional investment vehicles such as stocks and bonds, or alternatively, shift attention towards alternative investment avenues, such as real estate crowdfunding.

What is the Significance of Budgeting?

It is imperative for both businesses and individuals to establish a monthly budget to effectively manage expenses. The budget enables us to have a comprehensive understanding of our daily expenditure, thereby permitting us to evaluate the necessity of each individual expense and discern between essential and nonessential costs.

Nevertheless, a significant number of individuals are reluctant to create a budget due to the perception that it imposes constriction and an air of personal humility upon them. This perspective is misguided and detrimental as it merely serves as a means of evading the confrontation of this issue. Furthermore, a considerable number of individuals are afflicted by the phenomenon known as "compulsive shopping" (which will be discussed in greater depth subsequently), and being constrained by a constrained financial means is their most dreaded predicament.

What strategies can be employed to establish a comprehensive monthly budget?

Initially, it is imperative to meticulously scrutinize the expenditures accrued in the preceding months and endeavor to ascertain a mean value. Invoices and expenditures relating to sustenance. An average serves as an adequate initial reference for determining the initial value of our budget, namely the amount we will allocate each month as our fixed fee.

It is imperative to augment the original figure by including the costs pertaining to the unnecessary elements and unforeseen circumstances. Evaluate your supplementary expenditures and contemplate their necessity, discerning which ones you intend to conserve. Please remove any activities that you deem unnecessary prior to establishing your monthly budget, consequently eliminating a significant source of potential waste.

The monthly budget is not limited to covering only essential expenses; it should also provide room for unexpected expenses or indulgences, serving as a motivation to adhere to this financial limit. Ensuring that the cost remains within your monthly budget, receiving an impromptu treat such as an ice cream or an additional pizza serves as a fitting reward, thus ensuring fairness in the allocation.

Please refrain from regarding this monthly budget as an inflexible constraint; rather, view it as a framework to guide your expenditure. If you can not respect this budget for some reasons, do not worry, analyzed the problems that forced you to overcome your budget and assessed the possibility to increase it if these issues were to become constant. If, nevertheless, you are able to adhere to the budget, it is imperative to determine whether you have done so effortlessly or through making sacrifices. In the initial scenario, ensure that you adhere to your budget, whereas in the alternative scenario, consider augmenting it.

In the event that you are able to adhere to the allocated budget, it would be advisable to reward yourself with a suitable token of appreciation. Examples of such rewards could include indulging in a day of relaxation at a wellness center, having a celebratory cake, or engaging in a modest yet enjoyable expenditure, provided that it remains within reasonable limits. This accolade aims to foster adherence to fiscal guidelines and serve as a psychological impetus, a form of recognition for exemplary performance.

Chapter Two - Pitfalls of Minimalism

Upon careful inspection of one's dwelling, it is highly probable to discover a multitude of articles that can be deemed superfluous.

What is the purpose or function of all the adornments in your possession?

Is it mandatory to possess ten pairs of shoes?

Do you not believe that the quantity of food present in your refrigerator is excessive?

Is it possible for you to survive without a high-priced cellular device?

The aforementioned inquiries were the initial ones that arose in my thoughts, and in order to initiate the process of saving and following budgetary constraints, one must commence an evaluation of their expenses starting from their place of residence.

Initially, commence the process by enumerating all the superfluous belongings within your household and reflect upon the occasions of their acquisition, as well as any ongoing purchases.

This serves as an excellent foundation. Frequently, we engage in the act of purchasing items simply for the satisfaction it brings or due to our immediate preference for them. However, once we arrive home, these items often reveal themselves to be devoid of utility or usefulness.

The subsequent phase involves examining the expenses incurred outside the residence, such as morning coffee, confectionery items, social indulgences like drinks with acquaintances, and the cost of cigarettes.

These charges may initially appear insignificant, but over the course of a month, they can gradually accumulate and result in substantial expenses.

In this context, it is important to question whether these expenditures are necessary as well.

Would it be possible to indulge in an aperitif on a weekly basis rather than on a daily basis? Start to quit smoking? Less sweet?

Frequently, these habits have detrimental effects on our health, as we tend to consume an excessive amount of unhealthy food when we are away from home.

In practical application, it is necessary to meticulously scrutinize all expenditures and initiate a proactive campaign against any unnecessary or excessive consumption. However, it is imperative to note that this does not imply a complete avoidance of indulging in cakes or spending money; rather, it suggests refraining from daily expenditures on items that ultimately provide no real benefit to us.

This cost control operation is characterized by the principle of "Minimalism" as established by an individual.

However, what precisely does the term "Minimalism" denote?

Minimalism can be characterized as a way of life in which one endeavors to minimize wastage and eliminate superfluous possessions. The essential minimum surpasses adequacy for the sustenance of a standard way of living.

The benefit of this way of life, at least in its intended purpose, lies in its emphasis on prioritizing essentials and therefore conserving time, finances, and physical exertion.

For instance, refrain from purchasing a new mobile phone model every year as it goes against the minimalist philosophy of "we do not need." Additionally, practicing minimalism involves abstaining from adorning your home with superfluous items and disregarding trends.

Residing with the absolute essentials, employing solely the necessary discipline to cultivate the preferred way of life.

Delineated in such manner, the Minimalist lifestyle is highly appealing, predominantly due to its propensity for substantial cost savings.

However, there are numerous individuals who oppose this lifestyle, as it ultimately prevents one from fully savoring the pleasures of life and showcasing them publicly. Flaunting can be perceived as antithetical to minimalism, as it involves visibly and ostentatiously showcasing one's wealth and possessions to a wide audience.

Envision, if you will, occupying a fashionable locale and observing individuals within that space. Designer garments, luxury timepieces, high-end mobile devices, fine jewelry, prestigious automobiles.

This can be conveyed as a vocalized exclamation denoting financial capacity: "Behold, I possess the necessary funds, direct your attention towards me."

Those individuals who proudly display their possessions firmly hold the belief that minimalism is a lifestyle that only befits those without a permanent residence. They maintain that life is ephemeral, thus asserting their entitlement to openly showcase their wealth and influence.

On the contrary, The Minimalists posit that ostentation serves as a means to gratify one's ego and denigrate others, epitomizing a message of "My wealth overpowers your poverty, signifying your inferiority."

Evidently, as is the case with all facets of existence, there does not exist a sole "correct" lifestyle and an "incorrect" mode of living. Every individual possesses the inherent right to lead their life according to their own beliefs and values, as long as it does not infringe upon the well-being and rights of others.

Minimalism can be viewed as a ensnarement that restricts through frugality.

It is widely recognized that "the stingy" is often portrayed as a comical archetype in various artistic expressions (such as the character Uncle Scrooge in Disney), and in societal perception, they are regarded with a blend of sympathy and regret. Embracing minimalism can easily lead one to be perceived as exhibiting avaricious tendencies, and thus it is imperative to steer clear of this misinterpretation.

What measures can one take to prevent it?

Attributable to effective fiscal management. The budget should enable a comfortable lifestyle, with provisions for unforeseen expenses, while avoiding imprudent expenditures.

If you successfully create an appropriate budget, you can adopt a minimalist approach and refrain from being excessively frugal, as you will possess the necessary financial resources to pursue your desires.

It will become evident to you that you have achieved a financial plan that aligns with a minimalist lifestyle when you are able to set aside savings consistently each month. Numerous athletes have consistently echoed a sentiment in their memoirs, asserting that "the magnitude of one's earnings is inconsequential;

what truly matters is the extent to which one can exercise financial prudence."

Demonstrating consistent monthly savings within your budget serves as strong evidence of successfully embracing a minimalist lifestyle without exhibiting excessive frugality.

Furthermore, the principles of minimalism can be implemented into various aspects of one's lifestyle.

To what extent can one ascertain the authenticity of true friendships? To what extent can we exclusively characterize 'how many' as 'knowledge'?

What is the extent of unproductive activities in your daily routine?

By adhering to minimalism, you can carefully curate your social interactions, choosing friendships that align with your interests and possess genuine longevity, thereby avoiding unnecessary expenditure of time on individuals who exhibit no desire for your companionship. Genuine friendships in life are indeed scarce, and you may be astonished to discover that the passage of time has the ability to diminish friendships that appeared enduring.

It is preferable to cultivate a limited number of genuine and truthful friendships, adhering to the principle of "less is more."

In addition, undertake an examination of the activities that you engage in throughout the course of the day. Numerous activities prove to be unproductive. How many hours do you allocate to browsing Facebook? What amount of time do you expend on a daily basis engaging with your smartphone?

During that period, you have the opportunity to engage in studying, participating in sports, or pursuing activities that foster personal development.

Minimizing any wastage of time holds paramount importance, as the time saved throughout the day could be effectively utilized in more productive endeavors.

This does not imply that you are incapable of enjoying leisure time during the day; engaging in activities that distract and alleviate stress is indeed important. However, it would be advisable to ensure that these activities do not excessively consume your time. Alternatively, if this course of action is not taken, it risks devolving into procrastination, which poses a significant hurdle to the adherence of a minimalist lifestyle.

Step 3: Strive for Financial Independence

Achieving financial independence is a consequence of maintaining a firm grasp over one's finances, encompassing the essential practices of generating income surpassing expenditures, settling debts, and diligently setting aside funds to meet specific financial objectives that one is resolutely determined to make sacrifices for and ultimately accomplish.

In order to strive for financial independence, it is necessary to:

- Ensure the establishment of an efficient strategy for repaying debts - Implement a proficient debt repayment scheme - Foster a well-structured plan for effectively settling debts - Establish an optimal framework for the repayment of debt - Develop a sound and strategic approach to effectively pay off debts - Create an organized and proficient debt repayment plan

As previously stated, indebtedness does not foster the attainment of economic autonomy. To achieve financial freedom, one must diligently settle their debts and strive to steer clear of indebtedness entirely. One can achieve this by establishing a flexible financial plan that incorporates a proactive strategy for debt reduction. The expeditious repayment of your debts will result in improved financial well-being and enhanced financial management abilities.

Save with a specific objective in sight (while implementing automated deductions)

We called this saving-for-a-cause. In light of the aforementioned point, it is imperative that saving becomes an integral element of your budgetary plan. One has the freedom to allocate as little or as significant an amount as desired towards savings. However, it is essential to save with a distinctive objective in mind, as this sense of purpose will foster a stronger motivation to establish automated deductions for savings.

The primary reason for the majority of individuals not succeeding in saving is their lack of directed efforts towards a particular financial objective. When individuals make contributions toward a particular objective, such as funding a wedding, acquiring a down payment for their ideal home, purchasing their initial vehicle, or pursuing higher education, their determination to make meaningful financial choices and endure sacrifices is amplified. Consequently, they exhibit a more focused and determined commitment to taking concrete steps in their financial endeavors.

After identifying a financial objective that you are truly committed to, it is essential to establish automated payments for the determined savings amount—specifically, the percentage of your earnings earmarked for progress towards your significant financial target. As an example, in the event that you have made the decision to allocate $200 per month over a period of 24 months for the purpose of initiating your drop shipping/online business with a total investment of $5,000, we kindly advise you to issue an instruction to your bank, requesting them to effectuate the transfer of said amount from your checking account to your designated savings account on a monthly basis.

Once more, it is possible to allocate varying amounts of savings depending on your current financial circumstances, level of dedication, and overarching financial objectives. However, it is generally advisable to strive for a minimum savings rate of 10% of your after-tax income.

#: Expand your sources of revenue

The most authentic demonstration of attaining financial independence lies in the possession of multiple sources of income. With the presence of multiple sources of income, one can experience a state of utmost financial tranquility, as the potential depletion of one income stream would be compensated by the remaining sources.

One can expand their income streams by allocating their savings into meaningful ventures, such as initiating a business, engaging in stock market investments, or purchasing real estate, among other possibilities. You have the option of initiating a supplementary business.

#: Practice financial responsibility

Adhering to a lifestyle aligned with one's financial capabilities is an essential principle of effective money management and indispensable advice for achieving financial independence. Continually exceeding one's budget and accumulating increasing levels of debt will inevitably lead to a tumultuous and undesirable financial existence, devoid of the tranquility and security necessary for peace of mind in matters of personal finance.

It is imperative to ensure that your expenses remain significantly lower than your net income, allowing for ample flexibility in your budget to accommodate savings, retirement preparations, investments, and the settlement of outstanding debts.

Essential Measures for Attaining Financial Autonomy

Firstly, Establish Financial Discipline

It is imperative to understand one's expenditures and their corresponding destinations in order to effectively tackle financial challenges. Some individuals tend to ignore or avoid examining the monthly expenditures by metaphorically burying their heads in the sand. This sequence of events may elicit a sense of surprise, albeit it presents an opportunity to bravely confront and overcome your inner struggles.

If you have been residing on visas and covering only the necessities, this situation becomes even more disconcerting given the fact that you truly lack knowledge of the exact amount you are expending on a monthly basis.

Acquiring control over your financial resources is a straightforward endeavor.

It pertains to the act of spending less than one earns.

You must determine the inflow and outflow of funds in order to obtain a comprehensive understanding of your fiscal well-being.

Step 2: Enhance Your Earnings and Efficiency

A significant number of individuals believe that engaging in a profitable endeavor is the path to attaining financial prosperity. Undoubtedly, the task of accumulating assets is facilitated by a higher inflow of cash on a monthly basis; however, the true strategy to enhance one's total wealth lies in practicing frugality and maintaining expenditures below earnings.

It may be a truism; nevertheless, it stands as the pivotal, paramount, indisputable verity concerning currency. In order to extricate oneself from this predicament, it is essential to grasp the understanding that income does not equate to wealth. What are the riches? Wealth refers to the portion of your net worth (the value of your assets minus liabilities) that generates capital gains, income, and dividends independent of your labor. If one aspires to become a medical practitioner or a legal professional, it is imperative to commit substantial lengths of time after completing years of specialized training and advanced academic pursuits in order to earn a salary.

Conversely, if one possesses a diverse portfolio of private enterprises, real estate holdings, parking structures, car wash facilities, bonds, patents, mutual funds, stocks, trademarks, and various sources of revenue, they would be able to leisurely relax beside the swimming pool.

The inherent significance lies in the ability to maintain one's standard of living even in the event of physical disability or the inability to continue working in one's primary occupation. Furthermore, unlike an individual employed on a fixed salary basis, financial prosperity does not possess the ability to terminate one's position; it is incumbent upon the individual to squander it. It is considerably more effortless to jeopardize employment that nullifies a well-established portfolio.

The quantification of your affluence should be determined by the duration for which you can comfortably sustain your standard of living in the absence of supplemental income. If circumstances necessitated, what would be the duration for which you could sustain your current expenditure patterns on items such as cars, clothing, music lessons, tuition fees, video games, and the like?

The average person is not educated in this particular realm, hence their perplexity as to why financial freedom and security persistently evade them, seemingly beyond their reach despite their increasing wealth.

Step 3: Allocate additional funds towards savings and enhance your savings account.

Avoid being among those individuals who make statements such as, "I will commence saving money when..." The problem with this line of thinking is that the anticipated initiation never transpires.

The better position? At present, the time is now! The time is reliable. It is imperative to consistently prioritize savings irrespective of prevailing circumstances. That is undoubtedly one of the most effective methods to ensure continuous progress is achieved.

If you currently face constraints within your financial framework that prevent you from allocating funds, then the recommended course of action is to augment your income, curtail your expenditures, or adopt a combination of both approaches.

According to John Maxwell, one can only witness a transformation in their life if they modify their daily actions. The key to our prosperity lies within the intricacies of your daily regimen."

Tony Liddle, the Chief Executive Officer and Financial Advisor at Sark Investments, convenes with his spouse every January to meticulously establish the annual goals.

We have established a comprehensive operational and personal financial plan, incorporating specific monetary targets. Subsequently, in order to maintain accountability, we systematically assess our monthly expenditures. This ensures our adherence to achieving our financial goals. I would propose the establishment of an optimal framework that caters to your unique needs and those of your family. By merely documenting your objectives, you will be able to initiate the process. Regardless of the scenario, conducting daily evaluations and engaging in impartial discussions regarding your fiscal position will determine your success or failure in achieving financial independence.

Do not allow pardons to impede the act of saving money. The commencement of a far-reaching goal commences today and persists indefinitely.

Step 4: Allocate resources towards enhancing your financial knowledge and understanding.

In case you are a beginning investor, center around increasing your financial education – you will have to become financially familiar.

In order to expedite your success, it is advisable to engage in activities such as perusing literature, attending seminars, viewing instructional videos, and seeking guidance from individuals who have recently achieved the objectives you strive to achieve.

If you possess a higher level of knowledge as a depositor, it is imperative that you strategically expand your asset portfolio to a sufficient extent, so as to ultimately achieve financial independence.

In order to accomplish this at present, it is probable that you will need to undertake unconventional measures, distinct from those employed to attain your current standing.

Not only will it be necessary for you to acquire knowledge about more advanced investment strategies, but it is highly probable that you will need to surround yourself with a higher caliber of mentors and advisors.

Step 5: Diversify Your Investments

This reverts to the uncertainty surrounding the future trajectory of the business sectors. To safeguard oneself against unexpected surprises, it is advisable to diversify investments across multiple asset classes.

It is imperative to possess a substantial sum of money allocated towards stocks, fixed-income investments, peer-to-peer lending, liquid assets, tangible resources, and real estate in order to effectively manage a large portfolio. That will provide you with protection against significant losses in the event of a crash in any of those sectors, while simultaneously capitalizing on the advantages presented by strong markets, regardless of their location.

Also, do not get insane with your investments. Opt for investing in index funds for stocks, as they offer reduced investment fees and alleviate the complexity of capital gains taxes. Maintain your holdings in real estate investment trusts (REITs), which can be regarded as a form of land portfolios in essence.

Step 6: Diversify Your Revenue Streams

In a comparable manner, just as you would seek to diversify your investment portfolio, it is imperative to diversify the means by which you generate profit. The stability of both the economy and the business sector has diminished compared to previous decades, thus necessitating preparedness for enduring both favorable and unfavorable circumstances.

For example, in the event that you have a full-time job that occupies your entire day, consider embarking on the establishment of a supplementary business venture. Additionally, it will not only provide you with an additional source of income for savings and debt reduction, but it may also serve as a substitute for the employment you may lose during the upcoming economic downturn.

If you are a business owner, it is advisable to seek opportunities for diversification into supplementary streams of income. Please take into consideration the option of developing passive income streams, such as becoming an investor in a privately managed venture.

Several sources of income can independently indicate a form of financial independence.

Step 7: Strategize to achieve your goals

Develop distinct investment strategies tailored to your objectives, such as marriage, wellbeing, and education. Assess and quantify these strategies, and establish a specified time frame for their implementation. It is advisable to conduct thorough research and allocate sufficient time in order to make informed decisions, refraining from blindly following popular opinion, and dedicating effort and time towards understanding the fundamentals. Establish your strategic course of action to address the circumstances and adhere to it throughout the duration of your investment timeline. This will prevent you from making hasty decisions.

Step 8: Allocate all funds exceeding the stated threshold for investment purposes.

After ensuring that your emergency fund is sufficiently funded, you can proceed to approach the allocation of your assets with a rational mindset. This is crucial as investing involves utilizing capital to generate returns. As your investment portfolio expands, you approach a state of financial autonomy.

In an ideal scenario, your endeavors to save additional funds should never diminish once you have established your emergency fund. Rather than that, you should enhance your endeavors to provide further support to your investment accounts. It should become more feasible once you have established a contingency fund.

Chapter Four: Mitigating Fraudulent Practices and Initiating Beneficial Routines

In the preceding chapter, we acquired knowledge pertaining to various forms of credit as well as the two prevailing ideologies concerning repayment strategies. Within this chapter, we shall conclusively enhance your comprehension of credit matters by enlightening you on prevalent instances of fraudulent credit activities and cautioning you against potential missteps to evade. Additionally, you will acquire the knowledge necessary to cultivate beneficial practices that will guarantee your progression towards a more robust credit profile, thus perpetuating such favorable progress.

During periods of turmoil, there are occasions when we make unfavorable choices. Given the prevailing credit epidemic, it is unsurprising that certain unscrupulous individuals and enterprises seek to capitalize on individuals' poor credit circumstances for the sole purpose of monetary gain or perpetrating fraud. Acquiring knowledge is your most effective defense against these types of fraudulent schemes.

Credit repair scams are a prevalent form of fraudulent activities in the realm of credit-related scams. A credit repair fraudulent scheme arises when an individual or establishment asserts the ability to enhance your creditworthiness through the elimination of adverse credit history from your credit report. Naturally, they are incapable of expunging any verifiable adverse information from your credit report. In the event that there exist any inconsistencies or errors within your credit report as a result of actions taken by a financial institution, it is possible for you to independently submit a claim to the credit bureaus, without incurring any fees, with the objective of having the derogatory information eliminated. An additional prevalent strategy employed by these fraudulent individuals involves furnishing you with a completely fresh credit identity.

The concept of expeditiously restoring one's credit may attract individuals burdened with a woeful credit history; however, the reality is that these fraudulent entities are furnishing an unwitting party with a purloined social security number. Subsequently, when an application for a new line of credit is submitted utilizing the details furnished by the fraudulent individuals, the credit record appears untarnished. Nonetheless, engaging in such activities is flagrantly unlawful, given that the information presented by the perpetrator has been illicitly obtained from another individual. The aforementioned situation may result in monetary penalties and potentially incarceration for the unsuspecting individual who falls victim to the fraudulent actors. The most lamentable aspect of this scenario is that individuals willingly remunerate scammers, thereby subjecting themselves to exploitation, which not only results in a futile credit reparation effort, but also entails financial loss and potential legal ramifications.

Do not engage with any company that offers to rectify your credit history on your behalf. These individuals or business entities will necessitate an upfront payment. Additionally, they might advise against initiating contact with credit agencies, emphasizing their commitment to managing all correspondence with lenders. One more indication of concern is the possibility that they might instruct you to fabricate details on credit applications. No reputable service will engage in any of these activities. Moreover, it is imperative to note that, in accordance with legal provisions, all credit institutions are prohibited from disseminating false information regarding their services. In addition, it is imperative that they provide you with comprehensive disclosure regarding your legal entitlements through the execution of a written agreement.

An additional prevalent fraudulent practice involves a service or offering that guarantees expedited enhancement or restoration of one's creditworthiness. Similar to the deceptive practices observed in credit repair fraud, it is noteworthy that enterprises or individuals proclaiming the ability to restore one's credit or fabricate a non-existent credit history are often engaged in fraudulent activities. Frequently, these fraudulent schemes will commence by presenting you with a proposition for a line of credit. Nevertheless, the interest rates are expected to be exceptionally elevated, potentially reaching levels as much as four times higher than the average credit card rates. When individuals who have limited credit opportunities come across such offers, they frequently perceive them as their sole recourse. Once the accrued interest becomes unmanageable and they find themselves unable to fulfill the payment obligations, their creditworthiness ends up being adversely affected instead of enhanced.

The sole factor that has the capability to establish a solid credit foundation is the practice of sound credit habits. Establishing a strong credit history requires a considerable amount of time and cannot be achieved through financial means alone. In order to establish a credit history, individuals who have no previous credit records must ensure punctual payment of their bills and make applications for credit lines. Several prominent credit card companies offer account options tailored to individuals with limited credit history. Naturally, the initial credit limits may be modest; however, through the regular utilization and timely settlement of your charges, you will establish a credit history and witness an augmentation in your available credit.

Consistency is crucial when it comes to maintaining the correct trajectory towards establishing and strengthening your credit. Engaging in excessive spending and accumulating high levels of debt by reaching the credit limit on your accounts will never lead to success in credit management. One issue that arises is the tendency of individuals to perceive their credit card as a form of monetary resource with no inherent cost attached to it. If the credit card's spending limit was contingent upon the available funds in your checking account, you would undoubtedly adopt a distinct approach towards its usage. It is imperative that you embrace this approach in order to successfully attain and sustain a healthy credit profile. In essence, refrain from expending funds that are beyond your means. Although it may appear apparent, individuals accumulate credit card debt through the belief that they can spend their finances at present and settle their obligations at a later time. This is the perception that credit card companies aim to instill in your mindset. Keep in mind that their profit relies on the interest that is accumulating. The longer you delay payment, the greater their potential for profit will be.

If you choose to utilize credit cards, it is advisable to exercise prudent usage. If you have the ability to do so, refrain from incurring charges that you will subsequently be unable to settle by the end of each month. Consistently settling the entire outstanding amount of your credit card debt on a monthly basis is the most advantageous practice one can adopt in relation to credit cards. In addition, not only will it maintain a favorable relationship with your lender, but it will also have a positive impact on your credit history. In due course, this approach is an effective means of enhancing your credit score.

It is imperative to maintain a vigilant approach towards monthly payments, not limiting one's attention solely to the obligations of a credit card. It is advisable to complete the payment of all bills, including those for medical expenses, utilities, or monthly services, in their entirety every month, if feasible. Should you find yourself unable to remit the entire sum, we advise that you make contact with the lender or service provider to explore potential alternatives in the form of reduced payment options. This serves two purposes. Initially, it is a demonstration of goodwill that you are committed to settling your outstanding debt. Furthermore, it will serve to prevent the occurrence of a default on your account, a circumstance that, if left unattended, will undoubtedly exert a detrimental influence on your credit score.

In addition to ensuring punctual payment of all financial obligations, another advantageous approach is to possess a keen awareness of one's expenditure patterns. This will necessitate a comprehensive understanding of your income, debt, and objectives. In short, make a budget. Upon establishing the practice of meticulously monitoring your expenditures in proportion to your earnings, you will acquire enhanced proficiency to address your financial obligations. In addition, you will observe sectors where cost-saving measures can be implemented and financial prosperity can be fostered.

In conclusion, the process of regaining or establishing a sound credit profile necessitates a conscious understanding of one's financial behaviors. By exercising caution and refraining from falling victim to fraudulent schemes, one can significantly conserve both their financial resources and valuable time. Moreover, through the prioritization of efficient and beneficial methods for enhancing creditworthiness, along with consistent dedication, noticeable outcomes will emerge in due course.

Effective Strategies to Optimize Your Budget's Functionality

Maintain a Record of your Expenditures

I am referring to the entirety of your expenditures, encompassing even the minor ones that were mentioned earlier. Some of the major expenses like your rent are easy because you can remember them. It can be rather effortless, however, to inadvertently overlook the minor expenditures. In order to facilitate your organization and record-keeping, it is advisable to retain the receipts for documentation purposes, or alternatively, record the transactions subsequent to the day's purchases. An alternative approach would be to incorporate them within the category of miscellaneous items. This will provide you with a comprehensive understanding of the financial situation. You have the option of utilizing the envelope system in order to facilitate this process for yourself. However, should you have a inclination towards electronic transactions, you can duly allocate all the necessary funds for each expenditure item by means of making deposits into an operational bank account or undertaking transactions through a debit card. Subsequently, you will exclusively be able to make payments using that particular card. One can easily verify the statements to ascertain the specific details of their purchases, including the timing and location.

Update your budget daily

This is intended to assist you in remembering particularly the minor expenditures. One may utilize Evernote as a means to document their expenditures promptly upon incurring them. This measure will guarantee that there is minimal temporal disparity between the instance when the expenditure is generated and when it is documented. Utilize cloud storage platforms such as Dropbox to seamlessly update your document at any time and from any location.

Use Accurate Description

Rather than indicating the establishment at which you made your purchases, it would be more advisable to specify the particular items procured from said establishment. One can encapsulate this information by classifying them under specific categories such as apparel, provisions, or domestic sanitizers.

Adopt a monthly budgeting approach rather than a paycheck-oriented strategy

Due to discrepancies in our individual income schedules, it is advisable to adopt a monthly budgeting approach rather than basing it on the timing of each individual paycheck. This offers an extended duration, affording individuals the opportunity to initiate a fresh beginning with the commencement of each new month. Additionally, it is advantageous in the sense that any unfavorable month will conclude and become a thing of the past.

Plan for Occasional Expenses

It is advisable to allocate funds for various circumstances that may arise over the course of the year, particularly when operating within a stringent financial framework. You have the option to categorize these items as miscellaneous. Furthermore, an inconsistent payment schedule may pose challenges in effectively managing the budget. Nevertheless, it remains a viable option; you may endeavor to calculate the minimum amount you earn and base your budget on that figure. In this particular instance, should you acquire any surplus, it would be prudent to set it aside for contingencies.

"You may experience difficulties with your budget if:

It is overly complex beyond necessity.

It fails to align with your principles, particularly when opting to replicate someone else's financial plan.

It does not accurately depict reality; rather, it should align with your actual income and necessitate expenses that truly correspond to those you have incurred, as opposed to imagined ones.

It seems like a chore; make budgeting fun because that is what its purpose in your life should be. To enhance your happiness and fulfillment in life.

It is not achievable in reality; let us recall our discussion on adhering to the SMART framework while establishing your goals and budget. Reconsidering that matter will lead to an increased level of convenience.

Be flexible

Please feel free to explore beyond the confines of your budget. In light of the anticipated arrival of guests during a specific month, you may consider allocating additional funds for the purpose and granting yourself the freedom to do so. Please ensure that you allocate funds from a different expenditure that you are willing to forgo in order to offset it.

Have some fun

Please ensure that you allocate sufficient funds within your financial plan to engage in recreational activities. This is contingent upon the extent to which your budget is constrained. Nevertheless, it is not necessary to allocate excessive funds for personal indulgences; instead, it is advisable to allocate a portion of your budget towards activities that serve as a form of self-reward. This is the sole motivating factor that exists to facilitate the encouragement of increased work effort. If your financial constraints do not permit it, adhering to the budget can occasionally pose a challenge.

Spend below your income

Exercise prudent financial management by avoiding expenditures exceeding your income. You possess a clear understanding that annual holidays will consistently occur. Rather than deferring your major purchases until that time, it is advisable to gradually acquire the gifts throughout the year.

Avoid unnecessary debts

If an investment does not have significant long-term potential, it is unnecessary to incur indebtedness on its account. Possess the capability to discern these investments such as real estate or higher education. When making a purchase such as a vehicle, it is vital to understand that its worth diminishes annually. It is an endeavor that is not advisable to accumulate financial liabilities for.

The art of financial savings and effective budgeting leads to contentment and alleviates concerns.

One must not merely address budgeting in isolation from the topic of savings. The primary objective of budgeting is to establish provisions for unforeseen circumstances, rather than relying solely on each paycheck to sustain one's livelihood. Thus, what measures can you employ to guarantee your adherence to the defined saving plan in accordance with the aforementioned budgeting guidelines? What strategies can be implemented to enhance personal financial management and achieve monthly savings? Allow us to delve into some of those concepts:

Pay yourself first

The most straightforward method of preserving funds is to ensure their non-possession from the outset. One can establish a savings account and establish an agreement with their bank to initiate direct transfers of funds to the designated account. I discussed the matter of direct deposit earlier. In this manner, the sole financial resources that will be accessible are the sole financial resources that you are able to expend.

Avoid accumulating new debt

Make diligent efforts to avoid indebtedness, or strive to limit it to occasional occurrences, if at all possible. Only a select few among us possess the ability to acquire goods without incurring any form of indebtedness. We have developed an excessive reliance on credit cards. Nonetheless, it should be noted that the more time one takes to settle their debt, the greater the amount of interest accrued, resulting in a larger sum of money that will ultimately need to be repaid.

Set reasonable saving goals

It is more convenient to accumulate savings when one possesses clarity about the purpose of saving. Establish a clear objective and diligently accumulate funds to achieve it. Have you not observed the marked facilitation of saving funds for a matrimonial ceremony? Although you may accumulate certain financial obligations, you are primarily faced with the imperative of maximizing your funds. Begin by discerning your desired expenses, and subsequently determine the appropriate allocation for each expenditure.

Establish a time frame for your objectives.

Establish appropriate timeframes for saving. Instill both ambition and feasibility in them. The attainment of each objective typically serves as a source of motivation. When an interval of time has passed, you will acquire precise knowledge regarding the required sum of money that must be allocated towards your savings in order to fulfill your aspirations.

Commence the act of saving as promptly as feasible

The more your funds remain deposited in the bank, the sooner they will commence accruing interest. It is crucial to commence the practice of saving at the earliest opportunity. Proceed with this endeavor, even if it necessitates the smallest conceivable financial investment on your part.

Please contemplate making a contribution to a retirement savings account.

You aspire to achieve a seamless transition into retirement. The sole means by which you can accomplish this is to commence making contributions towards your retirement. It is essential to bear in mind that retirement funds frequently impose restrictions that can serve to preserve the funds you are accumulating. Put simply, you are only able to redeem it when all other alternatives are exhausted. This can serve as an excellent method for preventing the dissipation of your funds due to an insatiable compulsion to expend.

Do not be discouraged.

The process of saving can pose a challenge, particularly when one is facing financial difficulties. Continuously motivate yourself at every stage of the journey. There will be an enhancement and simplification of the process. Once you commence, maintain unwavering focus on the objective.

While you are in the process of saving, it is important to acknowledge that your expenses persistently require your attention. Presented herein are a compendium of beneficial guidelines and methodologies that will facilitate cost reduction, thereby enabling enhanced savings potential:

Cutting Expenses

Eliminate extravagant expenditures from your financial plan.

During our previous conversation regarding budget management, it was highlighted that engaging in moderate recreational activities is beneficial for one's well-being. It alleviates the sense of tediousness and enhances one's ability to derive pleasure from the acquired wealth. However, it is important to note that your budget should not consist of extravagant items;

rather, it should be limited to essential necessities.

Find cheaper housing

Seek affordable accommodations in a secure locality. This will enable you to allocate the funds you are earning towards other expenditures. One could potentially allocate these funds towards securing their retirement future or acquiring real estate, such as a house they intend to possess.

Avoid expensive addictions

Substance dependencies and other forms of compulsive behavior represent harmful inclinations that undermine one's ability to save. Several of these learned dependencies include the consumption of alcohol, tobacco usage, and involvement in alternative narcotics. Consider the adverse impacts they pose to both your well-being and financial resources.

Stay healthy

Medical expenses have the ability to deplete your entire savings in a remarkably brief period. It is advisable to avoid such an outcome. Therefore, exercise caution in your dietary choices and make every effort to maintain good health; this will not only safeguard your financial well-being but also ensure the stability of your budget. Additionally, consider actively participating in a medical insurance program. While it is possible to contend that one does not frequently fall ill, it is imperative to recognize that in the event of an illness, one's earnings are adversely affected due to the inability to work, and the expenses incurred for medical treatments significantly deplete one's savings.

Selecting Your Vehicle for Passive Income Generation

Genuine prosperity and economic autonomy are not typically derived from a solitary origin, or at least not frequently. It is derived from establishing a multitude of income streams, predominantly automated, that collectively amass to form a substantial income. Passive income is indeed achievable for every individual.

The majority of individuals lack knowledge regarding the concept of passive income and its creation, consequently resulting in a lifelong struggle to make progress despite consistent labor. The commencement of achieving financial success is predicated upon cultivating comprehension of passive income and its generation, and as one undertakes this endeavor, they will equip themselves with the requisite tools for wealth accumulation.

When it comes to establishing cyclic flows of revenue, the possibilities are truly limitless. There are numerous methods available to generate income, and by showcasing a modicum of resourcefulness, one can streamline the entire process. There exist two fundamental categories: Business Passive Income and Investment Passive Income.

Gaining knowledge on these two sources of passive income, namely business and investing, will equip you with the ability to identify lucrative ventures no matter their location. Indeed, once you acquire profound knowledge about generating passive income and familiarize yourself with the various approaches it can be established through, you will uncover a multitude of opportunities that may surpass your available time to pursue, ultimately providing you with all the necessary means for a life immersed in prosperity.

Do you prefer to engage in spending or investing? The majority of individuals have a tendency to expend their financial resources, whereas individuals who achieve financial success perceive each dollar as a potential investment that can yield greater returns over time.

When one allocates funds towards an investment instrument capable of generating substantial returns, the result is the establishment of a consistent and effortless source of income. By exerting diligent effort at present, alongside making strategic financial investments, you can initiate a cycle where your money will generate persistent returns.

Once your funds are diligently invested, you will no longer have the need to worry about them. You have the opportunity to allocate your capital into various financial instruments, such as stocks, bonds, mutual funds, money market investments, treasury bills, and acquiring assets that appreciate in value. Possessing rental properties and storage units can also serve as excellent means of deploying your capital for productive purposes.

Both investing and running a business can be excellent means of generating passive income. Passive income can be generated from virtually any business venture, and uncomplicated operational frameworks can be established and utilized by individuals across the board. This concept holds promise for individuals who aspire to accumulate wealth but currently lack sufficient funds to make substantial investments with significant returns.

There exist numerous approaches to initiate online revenue streams with minimal or no financial investment. For instance, one could initiate a website or a blog, establish an ecommerce storefront via platforms like Cafe Press or Amazon, or become part of a network marketing program.

Numerous individuals have amassed considerable wealth by developing and marketing their own educational products, such as digital books, which they sell through online platforms. You have the ability to replicate these actions and leverage them to establish diverse sources of revenue. Creating a mailing list has the potential to yield significant profits, particularly when one has ownership of a business and its own merchandise to offer for sale.

The Importance of Exercising Prudence When Engaging in Online Passive Income Generation

Establishing a reliable source of income that does not require active participation is increasingly being regarded as a principal objective among numerous online entrepreneurs. The concept of generating income through minimal effort drives individuals in search of the ideal online opportunity. While the Internet presents an increasing number of passive income opportunities online, it is crucial to exercise caution and remain cognizant of certain considerations.

Prior to legitimately generating income online, it is imperative to acknowledge that this form of earnings does not necessarily preclude effort or labor. The majority of available opportunities are presenting a more autonomous method, nonetheless, no enterprise can thrive without investing time and effort into generating that income.

To achieve a truly lucrative income, it is imperative to establish your business properly from the outset. The greater your success will be when your website, presentation, sales strategies, and follow-up system are configured to operate passively. This endeavor does not come without labor and it necessitates exertion, yet by adhering to the steps provided below, one can generate a more passive income.

Steps for Establishing a Passive Income

Establishing an online platform can prove to be the most challenging aspect in the pursuit of generating passive income. In order to minimize the number of inquiries, it is advisable to retrieve comprehensive information from the website. Simultaneously, it is important to avoid an excessive amount of information on your website, as this may result in the departure of your customer base.

The optimal approach to presenting this information would involve creating distinct pages and organizing them based on categories. It is succinct and concise, providing visitors to your website with the necessary information while offering them comprehensive details.

An essential component is the provision of a comprehensive presentation that elucidates the entirety of the system to visitors. In light of the advancements in modern technology, there is a decreased inclination among individuals to engage in reading. Video presentations and visual slideshows are available to disseminate information to your clientele. Majority of internet-based enterprises are willing to provide a complimentary one upon enrollment. If the aforementioned resource has not been employed, assuming it was executed by a skilled individual, alternative methods as heretofore outlined may be employed.

Sales professionals with expertise in closing deals are increasingly being employed by a growing number of businesses. The primary cause of inadequate performance on the internet can be attributed to individuals' lack of proficiency in effectively finalizing a transaction. A growing number of Internet-based businesses are employing sales closers as a means to enhance their revenue.

Implementation of a Follow-up System is necessary for ensuring effective communication and maintaining ongoing engagements. If one wishes to avoid individually contacting every website visitor, it is advisable to establish an email system that offers prompt and professional responses to each individual. It is highly recommended to actively interact with your customer base.

The most effective method to accomplish this task is by utilizing video or audio resources. You desire to engage with your customer base. Utilizing a subsequent system is an excellent method to achieve that.

Telephone Number - Acquire an additional telephone line specifically designated for business purposes. This designated telephone number is exclusively reserved for your business purposes. It is recommended that you provide a professional voicemail message to inform callers about the necessary steps they should take next.

The implementation of a customer follow-up system is essential as it demonstrates a commitment to providing exceptional customer service once clients have been acquired. You may establish a dedicated customer service desk or alternatively establish a telephone line for this purpose. Regardless of your current earnings, it is imperative that you attend to the needs of your existing clientele, as failure to do so would result in a short-lived tenure in the business.

The online sources assert the potential for generating a passive income purely by possessing an online enterprise. I must caution you against harboring the notion that you can attain the desired level of income without putting in any effort.

The internet and commerce have provided us with opportunities to generate income online; however, it is important to realize that despite the sophistication of these systems, creating a passive income still requires effort and investment.

Preserve Your Finances "

If an individual harbors intentions of settling prevailing debts, amassing wealth, or otherwise enhancing their personal financial circumstances, it is inevitable for them to acknowledge the imperative of accumulating more funds than their expenditures or losses.

Therefore, it would be prudent for you to direct your attention towards exercising fiscal restraint, ensuring that your expenditure remains at a pace slower than the rate of accumulation of your wealth. Put simply, it can be observed that the key shared trait among the most prosperous businesses, organizations, and individuals globally is their ability to generate a surplus in revenue as compared to their expenditures. Implementing a systematic financial plan, including budgeting and saving, will undoubtedly facilitate your endeavors towards achieving that goal. These processes demand conscientiousness and self-control; however, those who refuse to exert effort cannot attain financial stability.

Budgeting

Implementing a budget will enable you to effectively monitor and manage your financial resources. This segment will encompass the fundamental characteristics of a budget. To establish your budget, it is incumbent upon you to possess a means of monitoring your monthly expenditures and revenues. Therefore, it is imperative to retain your receipts, invoices, salary statements, and any other substantiating records pertaining to financial expenses and monetary gains.

Initiate your budgetary process by generating a list comprising three columns. Please refrain from confusing your three-column budget with the three-column bill tracking system that was previously discussed in the preceding chapter. Utilize the platform that best aligns with your personal preferences and lifestyle. Certain individuals utilize computer software, while others prefer to create budgets by hand on physical media, such as plain paper and a pen. Additionally, smartphone applications designed for financial planning and budgeting are also available. Experienced financial planners suggest utilizing a sizable dry erase board to accommodate modifications and fluctuations in variable expenses, thereby ensuring constant adaptability and maximal visibility of the budget. You may need to engage in the process of trial and error with various budget media options until you discover one that aligns with your preferences.

Within the left-hand column, please proceed to formulate a comprehensive breakdown of all your fixed expenditures. Your recurring expenditures are the financial obligations that you forecast to cover regularly, with consistent amounts due monthly. Illustrations of typical fixed expenditures encompass rental fees, property taxes, waste management expenses, healthcare loan installments, trade union fees, among others. Fixed expenses can be anticipated, inescapable unless significant life alterations take place, and recurring, either indefinitely or temporarily. As previously stated, it is imperative that you meticulously maintain records of all your receipts and invoices during this phase of the budget generation procedure. The precision of your budget hinges upon it. Once you have conducted a comprehensive evaluation of all your fixed expenses, incorporating each expense alongside its respective monetary value, proceed to calculate the cumulative sum of the monetary values listed. Proceeding downwards along the left column, maintain a space devoid of any information and subsequently record an entry denoting the grand sum of fixed expenses as TOTAL: $[Sum of fixed expenses]."

You may discover that you possess consistent, predetermined expenditures that transpire at intervals longer than a month, such as automobile insurance, dental expenses, and quarterly contributions. If such a scenario is applicable, it would be prudent to determine the mean monthly expenditure for these infrequent but regular fixed costs, in order to incorporate it into the overall sum of fixed expenses. As an illustration, consider a scenario in which you possess a car insurance policy for which you make two payments per year. In this case, you can ascertain the monthly expenditure for this policy by dividing the cost of a single semi-annual payment by six. As an exemplification, the disbursement of $630 for car insurance every six months would equate to a monthly expenditure of $105. In this hypothetical situation, an individual responsible for financial planning would incorporate a sum of $105 designated for car insurance as a non-variable expenditure within the designated section of their budget. Once you have diligently taken into consideration all of your regular expenditures, including those that occur sporadically, documented them, and calculated their collective monthly expense, you have completed the initial section of your budget, granted that you are not encountering difficulties in settling any outstanding debts.

Nevertheless, you may find yourself in a state of indebtedness. If such is the situation, it would be advisable for you to initiate the process of determining the necessary actions to settle your unsettled financial obligations. The budget serves as an ideal mechanism for accomplishing that objective. Initially, ascertain the desired timeframe for the expeditious settlement of your liabilities. In the interest of clarification, this theoretical scenario will consider your financial aspirations to encompass the objective of achieving a debt-free lifestyle within a span of twelve months. Under those circumstances, you would need to determine the amount of funds that must be allocated monthly for the purpose of attaining the objective of debt clearance within a specified timeframe. Therefore, it is recommended to calculate the monthly fixed expenditure allocated towards debt repayment by evenly distributing the remaining balance of your outstanding debts over a span of twelve months. Please ensure that you consider the accumulation of interest also.

The central column in your budget is designated for fluctuating expenses. These are recurrent expenditures that manifest with consistent and foreseeable regularity, albeit with fluctuating magnitudes on each occurrence. Typical domestic variable expenditures comprise utilities, groceries, fuel, leisure activities, and apparel. Exercise transparency while compiling your roster of fluctuating expenditures. Have you misplaced a monetary note while partaking in a game of blackjack on a certain evening? Incorporate this expenditure into the financial records. Perhaps you succumbed and purchased a bottle of wine. That is also categorized as a variable expense. Similar to the approach taken with your fixed expenses, ascertain the monthly cost associated with your variable expenses. Enumerate all of them and calculate their sum.

Subsequently, calculate the sum of the first and middle columns to obtain a cumulative total dollar amount that accurately represents your overall monthly expenditures. Please transcribe this figure in a bold font size so that it expands and fills the area adjacent to the lower sections of both expense columns. The aforementioned colossal quantity represents the benchmark you must surpass. This foreboding figure represents the threshold that your income must surpass in order to make substantial progress towards your financial objectives. A budget will help you keep track of your spending so that you might bring your total expenses down.

Lastly, proceed to the right-hand column of your budget. This ultimate column will encompass your earnings. In a format employing one horizontal line for each item, please kindly enumerate all sources of income that you have received or expect to receive this month, while including the corresponding amount in dollars for each. Please ensure that all potential sources of income are accounted for, encompassing but not limited to paychecks, gifts, alimony payments, refunds, interest, and rebates. Once you have conducted a thorough examination and documentation of all your sources of income in the rightmost column of your budget, you can proceed with the computation of your total monthly earnings.

To accomplish this, merely aggregate the values of all your sources of income collectively. Please include this sum prominently in a larger font size towards the lower section of the income column on your budget. Upon completion of the aforementioned task, proceed to promptly juxtapose the aggregate amount of your revenue with the summation of your expenditure. Is your aggregate income surpassing your monthly expenditures, encompassing repayments for current liabilities? In the event that this is the case, you are making commendable progress towards achieving financial stability. Alternatively, if your overall expenditures surpass your overall income, it will be necessary to make modifications to your budget in order to achieve a state of financial equilibrium.

For instance, numerous novice individuals managing their finances often encounter a sense of astonishment upon realizing the extent of their expenditure on superfluous commodities and services. Upon initially creating a financial plan with my future spouse, I found myself feeling rather self-conscious as I became aware of the considerable sums I was squandering on superfluous expenses, such as indulgent outings with acquaintances, unnecessary fuel consumption for short-distance travel, and even moderately priced alcoholic beverages. Fortunately, with the presence of a meticulously crafted budget, I was able to discern precisely how I was allocating my surplus earnings. Therefore, I discovered it comparatively effortless to implement minor adjustments to my way of life that would gradually enhance the equilibrium of my checking account. I continued to derive pleasure from many of the identical activities as before, albeit with minor modifications. As an illustration, rather than frequenting restaurants with my companions every weekend as was my habit previously, I would proffer the notion of preparing a homemade meal for my intimate circle of acquaintances. I discovered that the expenditure for feeding five individuals at home is marginally lower when compared to purchasing a single sit-down meal, encompassing taxes and gratuity. My acquaintances graciously extended their assistance and delivered a few essential ingredients to my residence for our customary gatherings at dinner. Additionally, I commenced engaging in skating, walking, or utilizing my bicycle for shorter distances instead of operating a motor vehicle. In addition to achieving savings on fuel expenses and vehicle upkeep, I also observed enhancements in my physical well-being consequent to those actions. I have also reduced my alcohol consumption. I would likely never have conceived of implementing these cost-saving modifications to my way of life had I not visually encountered my detailed financial plan.

To summarize, a meticulously structured and adaptable budget comprising three columns will facilitate your understanding and visualization of the origins of both your expenditures and revenues. It would be advisable for you to compute the totals of your fixed expenditures, variable expenditures, and sources of income in order to assess your financial management progress.

In addition, budget planners should adapt their approach as circumstances evolve. A budget is a dynamic instrument. It is not an inventory that one creates and subsequently disregards. In order to provide further elucidation, it is imperative to note that in the event of receiving a work-related bonus, it becomes essential to incorporate said amount into the corresponding month's earnings column. Subsequently, in the event that you do not receive it within a considerable timeframe, proceed to exclude said item from your budget at the commencement of the subsequent month. Proficient financiers make a point to consult and revise their individual operational budgets on a weekly basis, as recommended.

Saving

Furthermore, practicing frugality and setting aside a portion of your earnings will aid in the preservation of your financial resources. Accumulating additional wealth will be futile if you are unable to exercise the discipline of saving a portion of it. For the intent of this section, the concept of saving does not pertain to the receipt of discounts. As an illustration, numerous grocery coupons often feature promotional offers such as "a reduction of fifty cents" or "a discount of fifteen percent," among others. Naturally, the utilization of coupons serves as a practical means of financial management. Nevertheless, this section does not encompass that particular form of saving. Instead, the emphasis will be on the act of saving and retaining funds for critical circumstances. Failure to save money will result in a lack of improvement in your overall financial worth.

To begin with, a number of renowned financial institutions provide their clientele with the option of enrolling in automated savings schemes. An illustration of this can be seen in the Savings Today And Rewards Tomorrow (S.T.A.R.T.) program offered by U.S. Bank, wherein a fixed amount of twenty-five dollars is seamlessly moved from the customer's checking account to their savings account on a regular monthly cycle. The client possesses the authority to designate the precise day of the month on which this transfer takes place. This program operates under the assumption that the customer will refrain from promptly withdrawing the transferred funds from the savings account, as it is generally discouraged by most financial institutions to establish a connection between a debit card and a savings account. Please inquire with your preferred financial institution to ascertain whether they offer a savings program that aligns with your needs and preferences.

Secondly, it is advisable to incorporate savings into your budget, provided that you are capable of doing so. As you engage in your financial management pursuits, you may discover that you have surplus funds at your disposal. Although there is no inherent issue with indulging in enjoyable expenditures when financially feasible, it is challenging to dispute the notion that allocating surplus funds towards savings represents the utmost prudent choice. Therefore, take into account the incorporation of "savings" as either a variable or a fixed expenditure within your budget. For instance, it is advisable to deposit funds into your savings account to prevent immediate depletion. Therefore, the aforementioned funds are classified as an expenditure rather than revenue.

Furthermore, should you derive satisfaction from the ease and expediency provided by enrolling in a direct deposit program, it may be worth exploring the possibility of reallocating a fraction of your directly deposited funds towards your savings account. The majority of prominent banks extend the option to individuals who employ direct deposit to allocate a prearranged sum or proportion of their paychecks, received through direct deposit, towards their savings account, with the remainder being deposited into their checking account. You typically have the option to determine whether you prefer this agreement to occur temporarily or indefinitely. A single visit to a banking establishment has the potential to establish the foundation for a lifelong commitment to consistent and reliable saving practices, thus paving the way for a prosperous career.

Furthermore, substitute the settlement of outstanding debts with regular contributions towards your savings account. Upon the complete repayment of a lingering debt, you will find yourself with surplus funds as the previously allocated finances that were intended for the settlement of said debt are no longer necessary for such a commitment. One may utilize the additional income to repay outstanding debts and potentially minimize interest expenses. Nevertheless, once you have achieved a state of financial stability, it is advisable to redirect funds previously allocated to the repayment of outstanding debts towards the establishment of a savings account. One may consider granting oneself a modest incentive for the diligent settlement of said debt while concurrently accruing savings. As an illustration, suppose that in the preceding month, you successfully concluded your outstanding credit card debt by making a final payment of $200. In the current month, it is advisable to allocate this newly available surplus between your personal expenses and your savings account. One may contemplate allocating $140 towards savings while setting aside $60 for personal enjoyment.

Finally, it would be advantageous for you to allocate any additional, sporadic revenues towards your savings. For instance, if it is a prudent financial choice, funds such as birthday checks, bonuses received from work, presents, and earnings from miscellaneous tasks could be deposited into your savings account. Nevertheless, if you happen to possess an unpaid amount on a credit card subjected to a 25% interest rate, it would be a more prudent fiscal choice to allocate any additional sporadic income towards the reduction of your credit card debt, as opposed to depositing it into a savings account that yields a mere 1% interest.

The choice to allocate funds into a savings account may prove instrumental in determining whether one can achieve a financially secure future or face a lifetime burdened by financial hardships. If you find yourself overwhelmed by financial obligations, you may be understandably perplexed by the notion of depositing funds into an account designated for non-accessible purposes. The act of financial oversight necessitates the inclusion of both long-term and short-term strategic planning. Considering future financial planning may present challenges in the midst of immediate financial obligations; however, the eventual advantages derived from such foresight will prove highly advantageous.

One of the most considerable advantages of online banking is its ability to assist individuals in gaining a comprehensive understanding of their financial outflows. Having an awareness of the balance in your checking or savings account can facilitate making informed financial choices while engaged in shopping activities. If one possesses only a rudimentary understanding of the contents of their account, they are inadvertently creating a foundation for potential complications.

Every month, my spouse and I utilize online banking to ascertain our expenditures and the recipients of our payments. This serves to strengthen our budgeting efforts and enables us to make more astute financial decisions for the subsequent month.

One notable advantage of engaging in online banking is the capability to meticulously monitor and trace expenses, thereby enabling the avoidance of substantial overdraft charges. Please note, however, that in the case of the majority of online banking accounts, new account information will not be updated until the following morning. However, I have observed that numerous online banking platforms have recently incorporated this feature promptly. Presently, I receive daily notifications that indicate "PENDING DEBIT," followed by the corresponding monetary value. Subsequently, when it is published, it is published.

Children are truly remarkable, aren't they? Indeed, it is a divine providence that bestows upon us these precious beings who are wholly reliant on our provision for their welfare. It is our responsibility to procure sustenance, provide attire, and cover the costs of their healthcare. It is necessary for us to procure educational resources for them, acquire suitable sleeping arrangements, and ensure they possess a few playthings to engross and occupy themselves. Caring for a child poses considerable challenges, particularly when one lacks the knowledge and skills to effectively manage their finances.

Greetings, I am Derrick and there was a time when I lacked proficiency in effectively handling my financial resources. For a significant portion of my life, I devoted considerable time and effort to cultivating detrimental financial habits that had a persistent negative impact on me over the years. I lacked the knowledge and understanding of both saving a portion of my earnings and making prudent financial decisions. I consistently endured financial hardship, relying solely on each successive paycheck to cover my expenses. This was the recurrent pattern that defined my life until the birth of my four children.

I am the proud parent of three daughters and one son. Shortly after my youngest daughter reached the age of one, we were on the brink of being forcibly expelled from our residence. I was engaged in employment, however, I was not effectively overseeing the management of my finances. My former spouse, who is now an ex-partner, was also lacking in proficient financial management skills. Both of us would exhaust my paycheck in an attempt to cover all our necessities and desires.

We have acquired adorable baby attire for our children, as well as made installment payments for a high-quality automobile. We had purchased an ample assortment of quality items, despite diligently settling our accounts. The reality is that we neglected to exercise restraint in our purchases and persisted in acquiring items that held no practical value in our lives.

Furthermore, we did not accrue any savings. We lacked a contingency fund and additionally, we were devoid of any form of financial cushion such as an emergency credit card or equivalent safeguard. We encountered numerous financial difficulties and faced the imminent risk of losing our residence. It was at that moment of realization that I became aware of our lack of fiscal responsibility.

We had to change. I made the decision to seek assistance, although my spouse opted against it. The dissolution of our marriage ultimately resulted from financial matters, and consequently, I was granted custody of my children on weekends and every Wednesday. I recognized that it was incumbent upon me to provide sole support, resulting in a notable shift in circumstances. I would exercise restraint in my own expenditures as well as theirs. I provided them with the necessary items for their schooling and attended to their personal requirements. I have established an emergency fund that I refrain from accessing unless it is deemed necessitated. In addition, I ensure to engage in both financial savings and regular contributions to charity. I am convinced of the validity of this principle.

The invaluable lesson that my children have imparted to me pertains to the imperative nature of exhibiting responsibility when it comes to matters of finance. It is incumbent upon you to attend to the needs of children, as it is within your purview of responsibility and they are reliant upon your provision of care. I implore all guardians, irrespective of your individual circumstances, to strive diligently in fulfilling your duty of providing for your children, for it is incumbent upon you as bestowed by divine providence. Please deal with this matter seriously and make every effort to safeguard their financial stability."

www.ingramcontent.com/pod-product-compliance
Lightning Source LLC
Chambersburg PA
CBHW050246120526
44590CB00016B/2243